LANDFORMS

MOUNTAINS

Thomas Sheehan

Rourke
Publishing LLC
Vero Beach, Florida 32964

www.rourkepublishing.com

Photo Credits: Pg4 © Tony Campbell; Pg5 © Christopher J. Scott; Pg6 © Piotr Przeszlo; Pg6 © Hu Xiao Fang; Pg6 © Ianny19; Pg7 © NASA; Pg7 © NASA; Pg9 © Laura Lohrman Moore; Pg10 © USGS; Pg10 © USGS; Pg11 © Peter von Bucher; Pg12/13 © Marcy J. Levinson; Pg14 © USGS; Pg15 © USGS; Pg15 © Andy Z.; Pg16 © Beth Whitcomb; Pg16 © Igor Smichkov; Pg17 © Jason McCartney; Pg17 © Vasca; Pg18 © Ilyas Kalimullin; Pg19 © Stan Shebs; Pg21 © Paul B. Moore; Pg21 © Jakez; Pg21 © Gary & Sandy Wales; Pg22 © Bob Hosea; Pg22 © Mike Norton; Pg22 © Robyn Mackenzie; Pg23 © Andrew F. Kazmierski; Pg23 © Bruce Works; Pg23 © Joe Gough; Pg23 © Vadim Ponomarenko; Pg24 © Christophe Testi; Pg25 © Brandon Smith; Pg26 © Rafa Irusta; Pg26 © Ana Vasileva; Pg27 © James E. Knopf; Pg. 30 Illustration by Erik Courtney;

Design and Production - Blue Door Publishing; bdpublishing.com

Library of Congress Cataloging-in-Publication Data

Library of Congress Cataloging-in-Publication Data

Sheehan, Thomas F., 1939-
  Mountains / Thomas F. Sheehan.
     p. cm. -- (Landforms)
  ISBN 978-1-60044-547-7 (hard cover)
  ISBN 978-1-60044-708-2 (soft cover)
  1. Mountains--Juvenile literature. I. Title.
  GB512.S54 2008
  551.43'2--dc22

                              2007012290

Printed in the USA

IG/IG

Table of Contents

What Do You Know About Mountain Ranges?

Let's explore the mountains and mountain ranges of the United States. If you live in or near mountains, you, your family, and your friends have probably been enjoying them for years.

What? You don't live near the mountains? Then maybe you have traveled to them or through them on your way somewhere else.

This road leads to the Teton Mountains in Wyoming. These mountains were pushed up from the earth over a million years ago.

Do you know that a mountain is an uplifted part of the Earth's crust? Mountains often occur in groups, or mountain ranges. Mountain ranges are separated from other mountain ranges by lower and flatter grassland prairies.

Spring in the Wasatch Mountains.

Wasatch Mountains

Satellite view of the snow covered Wasatch mountains.

Maybe you know the names of some of the mountain ranges in the United States. How did mountains get their names?

You can find mountain names such as Pocono, Taconic, Wenachee, and Wasatch. These are Native American mountain names. In the last 500 years, Spanish, French, British, and other people explored and settled in North America. They called the mountains by names from their languages, too.

Spanish people, who settled California and the southwestern U.S. used the names of their saints; San or Santas. You will find the San Gabriel and Santa Ana mountains in California.

The Rocky Mountains

British settlers named the Berkshire Mountains of Massachusetts, and the Cumberland Mountains of Kentucky, Virginia, and Tennessee.

The Catskill Mountains of New York were named by Dutch settlers from Holland. The Rocky Mountains in the west got their name because when seen from the east, they appear as a great rocky mass. Many mountains have names that describe them.

The White Mountains

The Blue Ridge Mountains

Can you guess how the White Mountains of California and the Blue Ridge Mountains of the eastern United States got their names?

United States Mountain Ranges

Have you ever seen a **topographic** map of the United States? If you have, did you notice that mountains are often bunched together? Those groups are known as mountain ranges. You can find a list of them on the internet or on page 29 in this book.

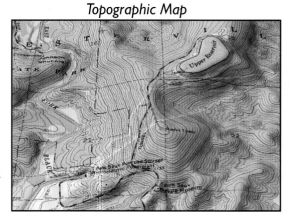
Topographic Map

The two largest mountain ranges in the United States are the Appalachians, in the Eastern United States, and the Rocky Mountains in the west. The Appalachian Range is a string of mountains that run all the way from Alabama to Canada. The Rocky Mountains in the west are a broad range and cover many states.

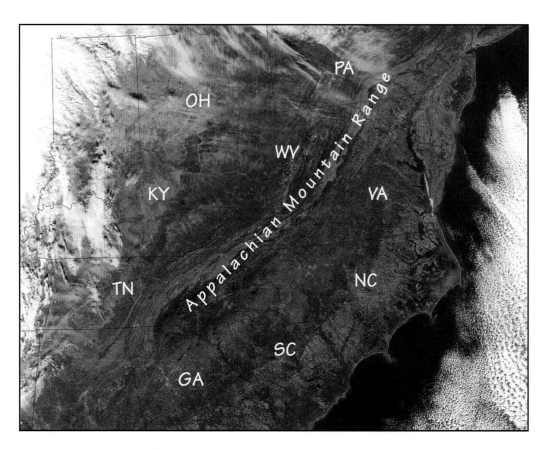

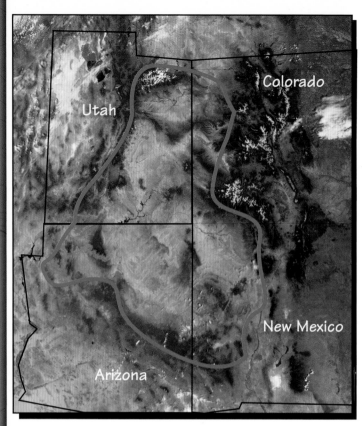

Seen from space, the Colorado Plateau is clearly visible and covers parts of four U.S. states.

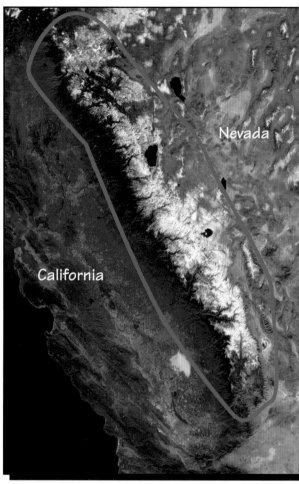

The Sierra Nevada Mountains run almost the entire length of California. These mountains are also known as the High Sierra Mountains.

Smaller mountain ranges are scattered all across the United States and North America. The Colorado **Plateau** (pronounced, pla - TOH) Range stretches over 450 miles (724 km). The whole range covers parts of Colorado, Arizona, Utah, and New Mexico.

Coastal ranges spread north and south along the west coast from Washington to Southern California.

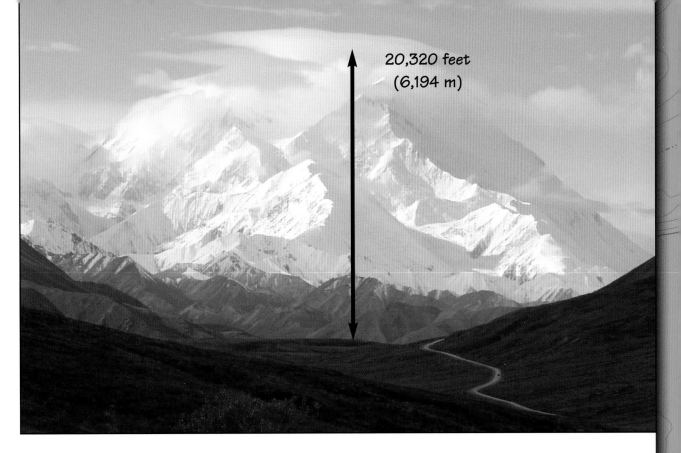

20,320 feet
(6,194 m)

Can you guess where the Alaska Range is located?
The mountain called Denali is in the Alaska Range. It is the tallest mountain in North America. How tall? Look at the picture of Denali. Can you find its elevation? That's almost four miles from top to bottom! Have you ever walked or run four miles? Can you imagine climbing that high?

Mount Denali is 20,320 feet (6,194 m) tall. If a set of stairs in your home is about 8 feet (2.44 m) tall, you would have to climb the stairs 2,537 times to go the same height as Mount Denali.

Have you ever heard of a mountain exploding? Mount Saint Helens is a volcano which blew up on May 18, 1980. Volcanic mountains, like Mt. St. Helens, often erupt.

It is one of several volcanic mountains in the Cascade Range. That range is in the state of Washington.

Mt. Saint Helens, located in Washington State, exploded with so much force that ash and rocks were thrown several miles into the air.

9,677 feet
2,950 m

Mt. Saint Helens 1980, before the eruption.

8,365 feet
2,550 m

Mt. Saint Helens 1982, after the eruption.

Satellite View of Mt. St. Helens.

Mountains also occur in an uneven or ragged line along the northern border of the U.S., from New York to Minnesota. They are part of the Canadian Shield Range. This range extends up into Quebec, Greenland, Ontario, and the Northwest Territories of Canada.

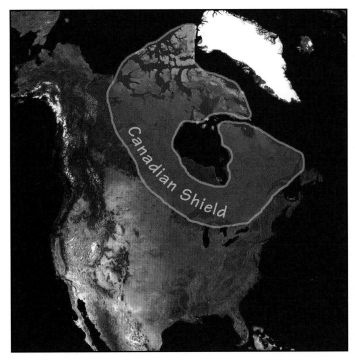

The Adirondack Mountain Range of northern New York State is also part of the Canadian Shield rock formation. There are about 100 mountains in the Adirondack Range. The tallest is Mount Marcy. It is 5,344 feet (1,629 m) high. Because the Adirondacks are close to many large cities in the eastern United States, lots of people get to visit them. Do you live near the Adirondacks?

The Adirondack Mountains of New York.

Have you ever seen Mount Rushmore? It is in the Black Hills Range of western South Dakota. The faces of four U.S. presidents are carved in the granite rock of this mountain. In 1927, the carving, using dynamite and jackhammers, was directed by a man named Gutson Borglum. When he died, in 1941 the project was continued by his son.

Known as Mount Rushmore National Memorial, it is located in the western part of South Dakota.

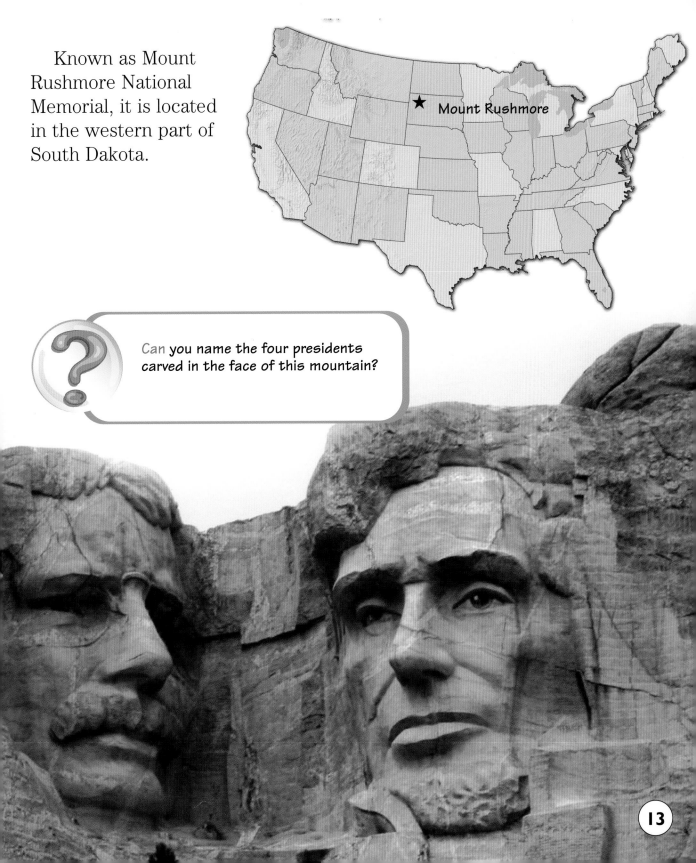

★ Mount Rushmore

Can you name the four presidents carved in the face of this mountain?

The Making of Mountains

How are mountains and mountain ranges formed? **Geologists**, scientists who study rocks and mountains, say it happened something like this:

The Earth's surface, or crust, is made of layers of sand and rock that can move around. As lava, or liquid rock, gets forced up from far below the surface, the crust gets piled up in some places and leveled in others.

The Cleveland volcano in Alaska erupted in 2006.

Under the solid tectonic plates of the Earth there is molten, or liquid rock, called magma. It comes out through cracks or weak spots in the crust as lava. Volcanoes are the result.

Lava shoots 30 feet up into the air from a crack in the earth.

The Hawaiian Islands are volcanic mountain islands that are continually growing and changing. If you ever visit Hawaii, you will be on the tops of the huge volcanoes that form the islands there.

Mountain Ecosystems

A squirrel eats nuts that have fallen from a tree.

Did you know that the plants and animals that live together in a place are part of an **ecosystem**? Each of the living things depend on the soil, air, water, sunlight, and climate that make up that place. If any of those things change, the plants and animals may not be able to live.

Animals use the plants for food. Some plants need the animals to spread the pollen that helps them to make seeds. Other plants need the animals to carry their seeds or bury them in the ground where they can grow.

In an ecosystem the plants and animals depend on each other to survive. We say they are interdependent.

Arctic Habitat

Tundra Habitat

Tree Line

Forest Habitat

Because the conditions of soil, air, water, sunlight, and climate change as you go up a mountainside, there can be several ecosystems on one mountain.

Temperatures cool, as you go higher. At the tops of some tall mountains there may be arctic conditions. Above the **tree line** it may be too cold and windy for any plants to grow.

Can you name the largest mountain range in the eastern part of the United States? See page 29 to help find the answer.

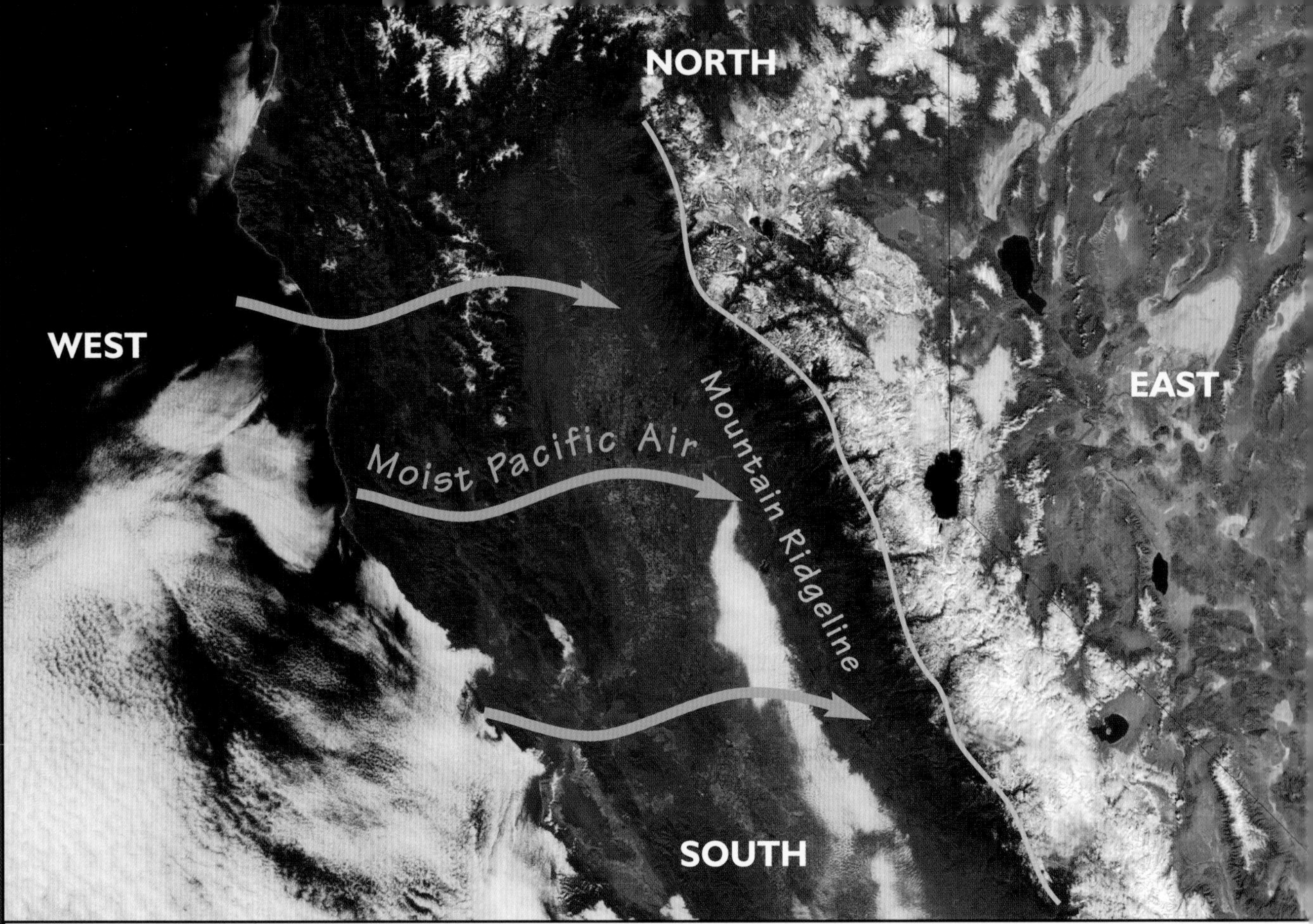

In the United States the three largest mountain ranges stretch north and south. As warm, humid air from the west blows across them the air rises. As the air rises up the western slope, it cools and loses its moisture as rain, as the air gets colder it turns to snow. The snow will generally fall on the eastern **slope** of the mountain.

This satellite photograph clearly shows the moist, rainforest, climate on the western side of the mountain ridgeline.

As air flows up the mountain it creates moisture which then falls as rain or snow as it passes over the mountain ridgeline.

The Saguaro Cactus grows on the dry side of many mountain ranges.

A marmot takes a peak outside its burrow.

By the time that same air mass travels down the eastern slopes, there is not much moisture left in it. Rainfall is scarce. The eastern slopes of the Rockies are very dry desert ecosystems. Here, water conserving cactus plants and sagebrush provide shelter and food for desert animals. The birds, lizards, snakes, mice, and other creatures avoid the dry heat of the day by hiding in burrows. They come out in the chill of the night to hunt for food.

Thousands of trees are cut down everyday in the U.S. to be used for making paper, furniture, and houses.

Mountain areas cleared of trees are called clear cuts.

Mountains and People

You are part of the story of people using mountains. Did you know that the paper in this book may have come from the trees that grow on mountainsides?

Are you wearing a watch, bracelet, or necklace that has gold or silver in it?

Gold Coin

For thousands of years, people have used soft and shiny gold and silver to make beautiful objects. At one time, coins were made of the gold and silver mined from the mountains.

Copper Wire

Copper Pans

You use copper every day. Copper is a metal that is found in the ground under many mountains. Whether you turn on a light, cook soup on an electric stove, or use a computer, copper wires carry the electricity. Are you using copper right now?

Enormous excavators fill jumbo-sized trucks, which take the material to processing plants, where the copper is melted out. What is left behind is mounds of material called tailings, toxic smoke, and scarred land. The cost of cleaning it all up makes copper cost a lot.

People also discovered that shiny and colorful crystals can be found in the ground on some mountains. Many prospectors have found beautiful gemstones like diamonds and rubies in the streams that rush down mountainsides. Many of these minerals are mined in the mountains.

23

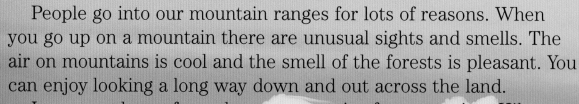

People go into our mountain ranges for lots of reasons. When you go up on a mountain there are unusual sights and smells. The air on mountains is cool and the smell of the forests is pleasant. You can enjoy looking a long way down and out across the land.

Large numbers of people use mountains for recreation. Hikers use mountain trails for the exercise and to enjoy the scenery. Skiers use the snow-covered slopes. Families build cabins, camps, and homes there, too.

Tent camping in the mountains is a great way to be close to nature.

People use the mountains for the natural resources found on and in them. Loggers harvest timber from the forests. Miners search and dig for minerals in the mountain rocks. All of these uses affect our mountains.

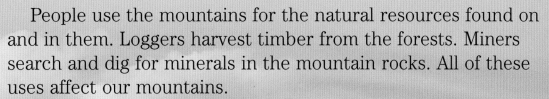

A young boy spends time in the mountains learning how to fish.

What Can We Do to Protect Our Mountains?

Road and home building, vehicle and foot traffic, and other human activities can change the mountains in ways that are damaging and harmful. Logging and mining on mountain slopes can cause rainwater and snow runoff to wash away the soil. Animals and plants may die when their ecosystem is altered.

When too many people use a mountain, their trash and sewage can spoil it. Mountains can become ugly and useless things.

All of this means that we need to be careful how we use the mountains, and how much we use them.

Would you like to visit a National Park in the mountains and end up stuck in a traffic jam? Millions of Americans visit our national parks each year. There are spectacular views of oceans, rivers, mountains, and monuments. They are beautiful places. But not when you are stuck in traffic, breathing exhaust.

All over the world, mountains are being stripped of their trees.

ADOPT-A-ROAD LITTER CONTROL

○ **County**
Department of Transportation
Road Services Division

Today, volunteers and professionals are finding new ways to protect our mountains. If we keep cars off mountains, we have less exhaust pollution. If people pick up their waste, we have less garbage polluting our rivers. People can cause problems when they use mountains, but people can solve them, too. Can you help solve these problems?

Cascade Range

Sawtooth Ranges

Rocky Mountains

White Mountains

Sierra Nevada Mountains

San Juan Mountains

Ozark Mountain Region

Boston Mountains

Appalachian Mountains

Blue Ridge Mountains

Adirondack Mountains

Green Mountains

White Mountains

Snow Line

Summit

Pass

Divide

Ridge

Slope

Cliff

Treeline

Treeline

Talus Slope

Foothills

Foothills

Gorge

River

Plains

Glossary

cliff (klif) — a high and steep face of rock

divide (duh VIDE) — a mountain ridge that causes water to flow in opposite directions

ecosystem (EK oh siss tem) — a biological community of plants and animals

foothills (FUT hilz) — small hills located at the base of a mountain

geologist (jee OL uh jest) — a scientist who studies the physical Earth

gorge (gorj) — a deep, narrow passage carved out of rock

pass (pass) — an area which people can use to go between mountains

plains (planez) — an area of land that is flat and has a clear view

ridge (rij) — a long, narrow section of mountain that has a slope on two sides

river (RIV ur) — a large, flowing body of water that leads to the ocean

satellite (SAT uh lite) — a device launched into orbit and used to take photographs and monitor the Earth

slope (slohp) — a slanted area on the side of a mountain or hill

snow line (SNOH line) — a boundary line marking the lowest point where snow comes down a mountain

summit (SUHM it) — the highest point of a mountain

talus slope (TA les - slohp) — a sloping group of rocks at the base of a cliff

topographic (tuh po GRAF ek) — the detailed description, or features of a place or region

tree line (tree line) — the highest point at which trees grow on the side of a mountain

Index

Further Reading

Tocci, Salvatore. *Alpine Tundra.* Watts Library, 2005.
Nadeau, Isaac. *Mountains.* Powerkids Press, 2006.
Royston, Angela. *Mountains.* Heinemann, 2005.

Websites to Visit

www.edu.pe.ca/southernkings/mountainmm.htm
42explore.com/mountain.htm
www.factmonster.com/ce6/us/A0842189.html

About the Author

Thomas Sheehan lives, breathes, and teaches science on Maine. He credits the English Departments at Cornell University and SUNY for awakening his interest in good writing, E.B. White's *Elements of Style* for smoothing out the wrinkles, and the editors at *The Bangor Daily News* for discipline.